A Very Cool Festival

by Sheri Reda

MODERN CURRICULUM PRESS

Pearson Learning Group

How do you cope with the cold and snow in the deepest and darkest days of winter? If you live in Sapporo, Japan, you go to an outdoor festival. If you don't live there, you might want to visit.

Every year people in Japan wait for the first weekend in February. Then they flock to the city of Sapporo, on the island of Hokkaido. It lies in the northern part of Japan. It's cold there, and they get a lot of snow.

For many years Sapporo was a quiet place all winter. Some adults went skiing, but most of them kept warm indoors. Children were the ones who usually went out to play in cold, snowy weather.

Then, in the winter of 1950, things began to change. On a cold day in February, some high school students went to Odori Park. That's the long, beautiful park that runs through the center of Sapporo. At first, the students probably ran around in the deep snow and threw snowballs at each other. Then they had an idea.

They began using the snow to make sculptures. Their excitement grew as they worked. They finished one sculpture and began another. Then they made more, and more. Finally they were finished. They had made six large snow sculptures.

The next day thousands of people in busy Sapporo passed the sculptures. They smiled when they saw them. Suddenly, the snow was no longer a bother. Instead, it was art!

The next year, people looked for new snow sculptures. They were not disappointed. There were sculptures that winter, the next, and the winter after that. Each year the sculptures were bigger and more beautiful. People made a tradition out of going to see the snow sculptures—or building one themselves.

The Sapporo snow sculptures became famous all over Japan. People came from other islands to see them. They began to come from other countries too. Finally the people of Sapporo declared a yearly snow festival. It would take place around the first weekend in February.

Over time, the festival grew. It covered three sites. Each site had food, music, dancing, dog races, and other treats. But the sculptures were the most impressive thing at each site. They made Sapporo sparkle and glow.

In 1974 the city of Sapporo hosted the Winter Olympics. People came from all over the world to compete in winter sports.

The competing athletes must have inspired the people of Sapporo, because they came up with a new event. It became part of the Sapporo Snow Festival. In 1974 Sapporo held its first international snow sculpture contest! Six countries competed.

Today, many teams from as far away as Australia, Canada, New Zealand, Southeast Asia, and the United States join in the Sapporo Snow Festival. They fly in from all over the world to take part in the contest.

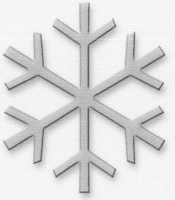

You might be surprised at all the preparation snow sculpting takes. Even the clothes a team wears are very important. It's terribly cold work! Sculptors wear long underwear, sweaters, snow pants, ski jackets, hats, and gloves. The streets of Sapporo are very icy. To be sure no one skids on the ice, the sensible Sapporans wear snow chains on their shoes and boots. Visitors also buy snow chains for their winter boots to prevent skids!

Some of the sculptors also buy a *hokkailo*, or body warmer. It's a small packet of chemicals that produces heat. They wear it between their long underwear and their clothes. It helps them stay warm while they build their sculptures. But the hokkailo can be dangerous cargo! Wearers have to move it around, so they'll stay warm without getting burned.

Once the visitors have the proper gear, they are ready to begin working on their sculpture. First they must get a cargo of snow down from the mountains. Sometimes they experience delays from snowslides or ice storms.

Then they wait for dark, when snow is colder and less likely to melt. Warm weather can cause more delays. Some of the contestants work all night, for many nights in a row.

Next the builders consult their plans. Most teams plan what they will build before they begin. Some create complex blueprints. Then they work from these blueprints, just as builders work from plans for a house.

Indeed, some of the sculptures are grander than most houses! One team built a copy of Linderhoff Castle in Germany. Another built a copy of St. Paul's Cathedral in London.

After they check their plans, the contestants build a wood frame and attach solid panels. Then they fill the frame with snow. They pack the snow as tightly as they can. That way, the sculpture will be hard, dense, and strong. They will be able to carve intricate details in the sculpture.

Once the packed snow hardens, the builders remove the panels. They keep the frame up, though, so they will have something to climb on as they work. Soon a work of art will emerge from that giant block of snow.

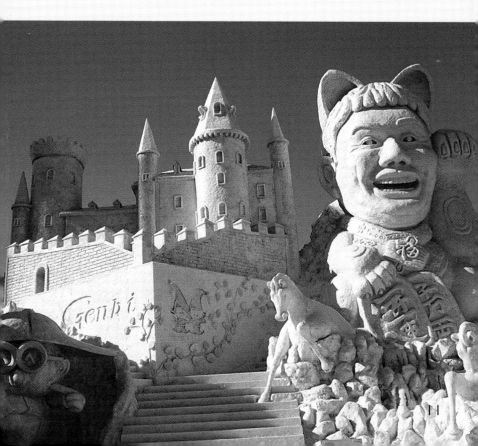

The builders climb up on their frames to carve details into their sculptures. First they use large tools, like hatchets and shovels, to do the rough carving. When that is done, they use carving tools and their hands. Then they add details.

Many builders have small models of the sculpture they wish to make. They use the models to help them remember all the details they want to add.

When the sculpture is done, the builders go over it again. They brush away fallen snow. They chip icicles off the edges. They patch cracks. They fix crumbled parts of the structure. Then they take down the frame.

At some point, they must decide there is nothing more to do. The sculpture is open for public view. Some sculptors will get acquainted with the other snow artists. Some will see the sights in Sapporo. Others will just wait for an announcer to name the winners.

Not all the contestants build copies of palaces and temples. Some sculptors copy famous places or popular statues.

Still other snow sculptors design and create original works. One year, a sculptor made a city bus out of snow and ice. People could even climb aboard it!

Other artists create sculptures just for kids and just for fun. The Self Defense base at Makomai has fairy tale sculptures, ice slides, and snow tunnels.

Still other artists make sculptures that don't represent anything at all. They are abstract and simply have interesting shapes. That way they can be anything the viewers like!

Some of the sculptures make people look through them up at the sky. That way they make the sky into a picture. Others make strange shadows on the ground. Some of them show what the artists feel or think about something.

Any way you look at it, the Sapporo Snow festival is a "cool" event. And it's a great reason to go outside in the cold.